T0196556

GLIMPSES OF HIS MAJESTY

GLIMPSES OF HIS MAJESTY

Anita Nyszik

authorHOUSE®

AuthorHouse™
1663 Liberty Drive
Bloomington, IN 47403
www.authorhouse.com
Phone: 1-800-839-8640

Published by AuthorHouse   06/08/2012

ISBN: 978-1-4772-0209-8 (sc)
ISBN: 978-1-4772-0210-4 (e)

THIS BOOK IS DEDICATED TO MY FAMILY,
EVERY ONE OF THEM A TREASURE,
EVERY ONE OF THEM LOVED.
A very special "Thank You" to my daughter Donna who is very knowledgeable in editing and on the computer. She was so willing to give of her time.

§

A number of years ago I purchased a camper. It was a chance of a lifetime for me. I had always loved camping, and because the owners were eager to leave quickly, I was able to buy it for an unbelievably reasonable price. It had a comfy wooden porch attached to it. There were storms and screens and a new wood-burning stove. I quickly moved in a recliner, a table and chairs, and lots of great books. Every moment I spent there was a real time of refreshment. I spent quality time in "His Word" and other Christian literature.

Soon, I found that I was writing down my own thoughts and feelings. I began to look forward to every weekend and the writing came easier. I finally realized that perhaps I should organize these thoughts so that others might be able to see "His Majesty" as my heart sees Him.

It is my wish that the reader would come to the full realization of the wonderful love Jesus has for him.

I thank Him often for my little home in the pines. I thank Him for allowing me to serve Him in this very small way. I pray that this book will bring glory to the "One" for whom it is written as well as allowing its reader to experience some very precious:

"GLIMPSES OF HIS MAJESTY"

§

TABLE OF CONTENTS

CHAPTER 1: For You Are "His Treasure" the Apple of "His" Eye... 1

CHAPTER 2: A Woman Said "Yes" to God................. 13

CHAPTER 3: Every Rose Is an Autograph From the Hand of God................................... 19

CHAPTER 4: It's Not Easy "Being Humble"............... 30

CHAPTER 5: He Came to Pay a Debt He Didn't Owe, Because We Owed a Debt We Couldn't Pay..................................... 37

CHAPTER 6: The Highest Place of All Will Always Be at the Foot of "His" Cross.... 44

CHAPTER 7: Was Resurrection an Endless Hope or a Hopeless End? 66

CHAPTER 8: "Nothing Costs as Much as "Loving" Except "Not Loving" 73

CHAPTER 1

FOR YOU ARE "HIS TREASURE" THE APPLE OF "HIS" EYE
Zechariah 2:8

I was banished from family, friends, and home. I was never to kiss the faces of my wife or children again, never to hold our new baby, for I was a leper!

I was untouchable. My home for the last eight years has been a cold, damp cave. I live alone. Oh, for a human touch, or even a handshake, but who would want to touch a hand with four missing fingers and a terrible stench? I kept it covered with rags so no one could see it.

It was getting difficult to walk now. One foot was missing two toes. It was completely numb. I sometimes lost my balance.

Every week my wife would leave food for me in a large basket about fifty feet from my cave. Today as I yelled out my thanks to her, I could see she was crying. All she said was "your face," and she left quickly. I knew what she meant. I could feel the sores on my face, also, a portion of my nose had rotted away. How I missed her, and how I would love to see my children again. This could never be. I must put it out of my mind and forget my former life. I had lost everything I loved.

There were others, too, in other caves. So many of them were much worse than I was. Many had even lost limbs, and the stench of those caves was sickening. At first I was nauseated. After awhile, my stomach became accustomed, as I realized that some of that stench was mine.

Others would venture out of the caves on sticks to look from afar at once was their land and their home, but they had to wear a bell around their necks so people would know they were lepers. They called us "unclean." I hated that bell. I still had some pride, and I'd rather rot in my cave than wear that bell.

I overheard the other people in the caves talking about a man who called himself "God's Son." They heard He had healed ten lepers. He would be passing by on the road just over the hill tomorrow, as He traveled from town to town with His followers. Wow, I thought, what a sick joke that was, but I found myself unable to get any sleep all night. By morning, I had decided to put aside my pride, put on that dreaded bell, and walk to the hill to see Him.

I reached the top of the hill and went down to hide behind a tree. A cloth covered my rotting face. I knew I looked terrible with dirty rags covering my hand and face and one foot completely wrapped so no one could see it was half gone. My smell was overwhelming. I could hardly stand it myself. I was even mad at God for what I was, and if I got the chance, I was going to tell His Son about it.

I could hear men's voices. They were coming down the road laughing and talking. They were almost fifteen feet in front of the tree when I saw Him. And—then they saw me. "Unclean, unclean," they shouted. "Go away." "Go away." But now He was close, and I could see His face. Others ran, but He stopped. He came toward me. I moved back a step. As I looked in His face, I saw no fear, no hate. He cared. He really cared. I could see the compassion He felt for me in His eyes. His eyes grew watery as a tear drifted down His face. Then I knew. I knew I had to ask. Lord, you can heal me if you will.

And then—He came right up to me. I couldn't believe it. He pulled the rag on my face aside. Then He took my face in His two hands. He touched me! He really touched me! Eight years without a human touch and—He touched me! My face felt warm, then He smiled into my eyes and said "Be healed." Instantly, I straightened up and felt warm all over. When I removed the rag from my hand, I could see fingers—all of them. His smile widened, and I knew He was truly enjoying my excitement. All of a sudden I could feel my feet. I hadn't felt them in almost three years. He looked down when I did and laughed.

He put His hand on my shoulder and said "don't tell anyone, but go show yourself at the temple and bring the proper gift for lepers who have been cleansed." My heart just about burst out of my chest with joy. I fell at His feet and put my arms around them. How could I thank Him? What could I do for Him? He pulled me up before Him and said "go now and present yourself in the temple." I could see that my joy was more than enough for Him and, reluctantly, I left Him. He moved on with His friends, but I knew I would never forget the love I saw in that face. His face would ever be before me.

I waited until I could see Him no longer, and then I ran and jumped and sang all the way to the temple and then home to my family. After eight years, I would see my wife and children again. I would plant my fields and repair our home. We would be a real family again. And—all this because Jesus passed by. What if I hadn't been there, or what if I had hidden myself and let Him pass by because of my pride? He healed me, but most of all—HE TOUCHED ME! Untouchable? Jesus didn't think so.

The next time Jesus passes by, will your pride let you pass Him by? I hope not. Jesus would see this man again. He would see him crying at the foot of His cross!

> Life is so swift, and the pace is too great.
> We dare not pause for we might be late.
> For our next appointment that means so much,
> We are willing to brush off the Savior's touch.

Jesus lives in us. We are His hands. We are His voice. We cannot serve Him unless we extend our hands to others. No one is saying it's easy to love people who are hurtful or unkind, who are angry at the world, who are constantly negative, or who take pleasure in verbally abusing others. In being only one person, how can we possibly make any difference at all?

- In a smile when we don't feel like smiling
- In taking time to listen when our schedule is stressing us out
- In showing genuine concern and in being compassionate

- In giving to others who are in need from our own storage house
- In asking Jesus to help us be lovable to those who are unlovable

And—In never giving up! Jesus never gave up. I'm sure there were plenty of times that he wanted to, but He never did. Such sadness, how he loved His own people, and how they openly rejected Him. But—He loved them even still.

Jesus saw something worthwhile in everyone. Remember the leper? No one would come within one hundred feet from him, but Jesus did. He touched his hands (or what was left of them), He touched his flesh-eaten face. Jesus took the time. Can you imagine being this leper who hadn't been touched in years? Just Jesus' touch was enough, but Jesus healed him too. Everyone mattered to Him. He paid a terrible price to prove it.

Even the criminal suffering on the cross next to Him was important to Him. Jesus saw the goodness in this man and allowed him to be the first person to enter His kingdom. Compassion, Forgiveness, Love, Jesus cornered the market. He had it all. And—He gave it all.

Did Jesus ever cry? We know He cried over His beloved city of Jerusalem and it's occupants, and He wept at the tomb of His dead friend Lazarus.

Can you see a tear running down His precious face for each of His little ones that are aborted? There is nothing to be said and—so He cries. What is happening to the human race? What ever happened to morals or standards? Doesn't a human life have any value? Does it have any worth at all?

God sees us differently. He sees a child that He has made. Every one of us is distinctly unique. Every one of us is valuable. We are His children, His most precious treasures. As a matter of fact, each one of us is "The apple of His eye."

He doesn't care if you're beautiful, talented or rich. Why would Jesus care about wealth when He's walking on streets of gold? Young or old, healthy or handicapped, to Jesus you are valuable just as you are. With all your faults and all your problems, your poverty, your aches and pains, your likes and dislikes, to Him you are valuable just as you are. Reach up and take His hand and you'll find Him waiting to take yours. How eager He is to welcome you, for you are His very precious treasure and—now you've come home. What joy is yours! What joy is His!

HE GAVE HIS LIFE TO READ GOD'S WORD

Many years ago in Russia lived a man, who in his younger years had secretly seen three pages from the Gospel of John. Bibles were outlawed at the time. Anyone caught with one or having been known to see even a small portion of one could lose their life. A good friend had shown the pages to him and then carefully hid them away, but Olaf never forgot how those words burned in his heart. He tried to remember them, but it was so many years ago. He and his wife were now old and sick.

One day the town's baker stopped by with a loaf of bread and some very exciting news. He talked in a whisper so as not to be heard by Olaf's neighbors. He told of a missionary coming to another town, bringing with him a whole copy of the New Testament. Olaf and his wife held their breath with excitement, but with sadness too, because the town was forty miles away. There was no transportation and winter was well on its way. The baker told Olaf that the testament had been given to the priest in the church, and he was trying secretly to show it to anyone who cared to see it. Olaf cared! His heart burned inside him. He wanted so badly to see those precious words.

A week went by, and Olaf didn't say much. He knew that his wife was too sick to make the journey, but he also knew that he must go. He had waited all his life. He just had to try. His wife could feel his excitement, and went ahead to prepare him for the trip. She packed him one large cheese, the bread from the baker, and some dried fish. He dressed warmly in his heavy jacket, his warm knitted hat, and his old sturdy boots. His wife made him wear two pairs of socks to keep his feet warm.

At the first break of sunlight, he kissed his wife and started off. Forty miles, he said to himself, but it will be worth it just to read the words of his God. As he walked, the sky grew dark. Olaf started to feel the cold. He tried walking as fast as he could. He hoped to be there in two days. He was fast becoming short of breath. He sat down under a tree and ate some of the lunch his wife had packed him. He felt a little better, but he was so busy eating lunch that he didn't notice the snowflakes falling all around him. It was only early afternoon and he had so many more miles to go. He began walking faster and faster and the snow fell harder and thicker.

He was well into the countryside where homes were scattered and scarce. He was overtired now, and his heart was beating faster. Hadn't the doctor warned him about this? But Olaf was determined. He had to hold those words in his hands and press them to his heart.

Feeling weaker, he found some large bushes and climbed under them. He took out the extra blanket his wife had packed in the bottom of his sack and fell asleep. When he awoke, it was still snowing. It was a thick, heavy snow with already one foot on the ground. He felt tired and weak. He ate some bread and cheese hoping this would bring him some energy.

He set out for the town. He should be there by nightfall if he hastened his pace. Oh! How heavy the snow was trying to lift his boots in and out of it. Much of the terrain was uphill now. He sat a moment on a fallen tree trunk. The heaviness in his chest was slowly beginning to return. Just up and over the hill now, but it felt like a million miles to him. He continued up the hill feeling weak and in pain. It was getting hard to breathe now. He finally reached the top of the hill where he looked down at the town. He scanned the streets and finally found the little church steeple. He could hardly get down the hill, but he pushed himself on. He banged on the door hoping the priest would still be awake. The priest saw how weak and tired this old man was. He warmed him by the fireplace and brought him some hot tea. Olaf told him why he had come. He told the priest that the baker had sent him.

The priest took him into the basement, which held a tiny room in one corner. He sat Olaf in a chair in front of a small table. He removed a block of stone from the wall and gently lifted out the book. Olaf gasped as he clutched the book to his chest. His dream had come true. He gently touched each page as he read on and on. This time he would be able to read the entire book of John. The look on his face was one of sheer ecstasy. He read on through the night. This Jesus, how gentle, how loving. He came to die and save us, and only because He loved us so much. Olaf had never read anything so wonderful. He fell asleep thanking God over and over for loving him.

The priest came to get him in the morning. He planned on preparing Olaf a nice warm breakfast before letting him return home. Olaf had fallen asleep with his hands on the book. The priest tried to wake him to no avail. Olaf was dead. He had died of a worn out heart while he was sleeping, but—on his face was the most peaceful smile. The priest knew this smile. It was the unmistakable smile of pure joy.

Just as Jesus gave His life for us, Olaf had given his life to read God's word. He considered being able to read His Word the most treasured gift he could ever receive.

Is the bible that important to you? Some people go through life without even owning one. Where do you fit in? Is it just a book that sits on the table and catches dust or do we leave it there to only impress others? God has sent us a precious "love letter".

IN GOD'S WORKS WE SEE HIS HAND, BUT IN HIS WORD WE SEE HIS HEART!

Psalms 16:11 tells us that, "In His presence is fullness of joy." We can feel His presence through His word. The bible is like holding God in your hands. He is speaking to you. In your lap sits pure gold. "Be still and know that I am God." Psalms 46:10

How can we define "JOY?" Is it a state of peace, or a personality that is always bubbly? Joy goes deeper than that. It doesn't mean that we are exempt from showing sadness or having to shed a tear or two when necessary. Joy is a quiet peace in the heart of the believer. Sometimes it manifests itself in a song while driving. Sometimes a person is so overwhelmed by the beauty of nature, a sunset, a snow-covered mountain that tears fall from his eyes. For me it has always been trees. My love for trees began when I was a child. It still astounds me when I look at a hillside and see the hundreds of different colors of greens. He could have made them all one color, but He knew we would enjoy them all. Often, it's just a feeling of calm when everything around you is in turmoil. "JOY" is contagious. You can catch it in His "Word."

§

A TASTE OF JOY

Joy is waking unto another day.
Looking into the faces of your loved ones once again,
Looking out on autumn's colorful gift,
Or waking up to a wintry crystal world.
Joy is seeing the result of prayer in the lives of those
you've prayed for.
Joy is knowing you can go to your heavenly father
with all your problems.

Joy is knowing you need not do a single thing to inherit
eternal life.
Jesus has already done it all for you on the cross.

JOY IS KNOWING WHERE YOU'RE GOING!!

§

Those who waited in such long lines believing He could heal them knew joy. Jesus always put His tired needs aside as He met the needs of others. So many others, so long a line, so many hurts, so much pain, such deep sadness, but—after so many hours of waiting—SO MUCH JOY!

Can you even imagine:

A child who was never able to speak calling his mother "MAMA?" Can you see her tears of joy? Can you see the look of amazement on his face, he was going to have fun with his new gift. Jesus was having fun too.

A blind woman, blind from birth, given her sight and finally being able to see her children? There were floods of tears, wetting Jesus' hair, falling on His robe and onto His feet. Jesus didn't care. Why, He was laughing and crying right along with her. She would be able to thank Him again, through her tears, as He carried that huge wooden cross up the hill to Calvary.

§

My Dearest Jesus:

A day without you is like a world without trees or flowers.

A day with nothing but loneliness,

A day that leaves a feeling of emptiness inside,

A day full of nothingness,

An ocean without water,

Movement without feeling,

A day completely void of joy,

A day without you, Lord, is just not worth living!

CHAPTER 2

A WOMAN SAID "YES" TO GOD

It was very humbling being a woman in Jesus' time. In reality, women were regarded as a lower form of life. Even the animals in the family held a higher status. Women were looked on so unfavorably, that even in the temple they were not permitted to go beyond a certain area, and they were not allowed to worship alongside their husbands in the temple. We've come a long way since then, haven't we?

But God regarded them so favorably and loved them so much that He chose to send His beloved son into the world through a woman, a young teenager. Being God, He could have sent His son in any number of ways and much more royally. He could have chosen a castle instead of a stable-cave. He could have provided royal attendants instead of the stable animals. He could have provided a crib of gold instead of the animal feeding trough but, instead, He chose a humble and obedient teenager who said "yes" to the angel Gabriel. Through her, heaven would come to earth. "Don't be frightened, Mary," the angel told her, "for God has decided to wonderfully bless you!" "And behold, you will conceive in your womb, and bare a son, and you shall name him Jesus." Luke 1:30-31

§

HUMBLY "HE" CAME TO THE WORLD "HE" CREATED!

Women were among those who befriended Him during His short life on earth. Mary and Martha were two women who had a tremendous impact on His life. They were two sisters, who along with their brother Lazarus, often took Jesus, along with His disciples, into their home and fed them. Occasionally, when the weather was bad, Jesus and His friends were invited to stay the night so they could escape the dampness and the cold. Perhaps Mary and Martha even washed their clothes for them. Unfortunately, the bible doesn't tell us.

Do you love to have company over for dinner? I do. First I decide what I will cook. Then I formulate my shopping list. Next, I set about cleaning the house until it sparkles. I always make sure the dinner table is set to perfection.

After my shopping trip, I begin cooking. Now, right about this time, I become completely exhausted and grateful for any help of any kind. Sometimes when our guests arrive, I am so tired that I find it difficult to enjoy their precious company.

Suddenly, reality sets in, and I realize with sadness, that I am a "Martha" and a person that I really don't want to be. When Jesus and His friends came to visit, Martha always ran around in a bit of frenzy preparing and serving while Mary sat quietly at Jesus' feet absorbing every word. Maybe Martha felt sorry for herself. Maybe she was having herself a pity party. She was angry with Mary for not sharing her part of the work. And, it didn't help a bit when Jesus told Martha that Mary was doing the right thing. "Martha, Martha," Jesus said: "Martha, dear friend, you are so upset over all of these details! There is really only one thing worth being concerned about. Mary has discovered it and I won't take it away from her!" Luke 10:41-42

Did Martha feel left out or even more angry at Mary? After all, wasn't she helping to feed Jesus and His friends? Mary knew that what Jesus had to say was far more important than anything she could do in that kitchen.

Please, Lord, let me always be a Mary and not a Martha. Let me always put you in first place.

- Before a clean house,
- Before trying to be the perfect cook and hostess,
- Before trying to impress.

Let me only care about impressing you, Lord, and teach me how to put other things aside so that I may always put you first in my life.

WOMEN WERE IMPORTANT TO JESUS

A funeral procession filled Jesus with so much compassion, that He gave a woman back her dead son. Jesus knew she was now alone, and He restored her dead son to life again. Can you imagine her joy? Can you just see Jesus smiling down at her as she kissed his tear-stained hand in thankfulness?

A woman weakened physically from years of hemorrhaging. She believed Jesus could help her. She thought, "If I can only touch the hem of His robe, I know I will be healed." She cautiously came behind him and grasped the bottom of his robe. Jesus knew, for he felt energy go out of him. He took compassion on her and healed her instantly. He then praised her for her faith in Him.

Women who believed in Him, followed Him and ministered to His needs. They brought Him food, and even offered what little money they had. Maybe they sewed or mended His and the disciples clothes. How grateful Jesus must have been to these women.

"Unconditional Love" was Jesus' specialty. Even a prostitute was valuable in His eyes. The penalty was death by stoning, a horrible and painful death. Mary had been caught in the act of her sin. She knew what awaited her, as the crowd threw her at Jesus' feet loudly demanding what He thought they should do. The stones were all ready and waiting in their hands. The crowd was trying to snare Him and He knew it!

With love and pity He looked down at her cowering at His feet, then He bent down and, quietly with His finger, began writing in the dust. What was it He was writing? The bible doesn't tell us, but I often wonder if it might have been something like this:

- Selfishness
- Lying
- Hatred
- Adultery
- Murder

- Stealing
- Envy

Did the crowd see these things He wrote? Because one by one they all threw down their stones as Jesus said, "Let him who has never sinned cast the first stone." They were all well aware of their sins and their guilt turned them away. As a matter of fact, Jesus was the only one in that crowd who had the right to throw a stone, for only He was without sin.

He lovingly looked down at Mary, gently lifted her up to face Him, and told her to, "go and sin no more." The crowd had thrown her at Jesus "as she was", and Jesus accepted her "as she was."

You, too, can come to Him just as you are, right where you are, and He will forgive you too!

It was a woman who wiped His blood-smeared face as He carried His cross up the hill to Calvary. It was the women who were unafraid to follow Him to the cross while almost all of His friends had deserted Him in fear. It was the women who wept bitterly as they watched His precious blood running down the cross.

And—did a woman weave the seamless robe the soldiers were gambling for at the foot of His cross? It was seamless, and it was considered to be such a treasure. Perhaps His mother made it for Him, or perhaps it was a woman whose child He had once healed. The bible doesn't tell us.

It was women who came early on Easter morning with extra spices to properly prepare His body for burial, but His body wasn't there, and to a woman went the honor of being the first to witness Him in

His Resurrection body. Did Jesus consider women favorably? You can be sure He did!

And—one more thing Lord. Thank you for making me a WOMAN!

CHAPTER 3

EVERY ROSE IS AN AUTOGRAPH
FROM THE HAND OF GOD

Daily He shows us who He is, from sunrise to sunset and far into the night with His sky full of diamonds, his moon and His galaxies, all of this in one single day. You can almost hear Him say, "Did you see it? Did you notice the sunrise I made for you? Why, I added that darker shade of crimson just for you. And—did you notice the crocuses coming up in your garden? I guarded them well for you all winter. Don't forget to look at your apple tree. I made sure that the blossoms were twice as beautiful this year. I hope you won't miss it, my child. Have you noticed how green the trees have become this week? I made them many more shades of green just for your enjoyment, and some of these shades you have never seen before. Did you notice the size of the waves washing in on the beach during last week's squall, why, they were absolutely magnificent. I remember how you wanted to live near the beach so you could see them. I try so hard to please you, my child, and I know you are busy, but if you could just take a moment"—So many miracles every day, and He loves us so much that He never tires of showing them to us. Do we even notice them as being miracles?

- A kiss from your child
- A precious newborn baby
- Looking out on the vast spanse of the ocean
- Seashore magic, like that perfectly rounded rock that was washed over by a countless number of waves for thousands of years. It was too perfect to leave behind. I took it home.
- Shells of so many colors and shapes just sitting and waiting for you to enjoy.
- His thunder and lightning, so awesome and so majestic
- Autumn hillsides so majestically colorful that our eyes cannot seem to behold that much beauty

§

Miracles, miracles, every day,
God wants to take our sadness away.
But how many times do we even see
the beauty He's made for you and me?
The sun, the stars, the gorgeous blue sky
and those funny seagulls flying by.
The trees, all sizes and so many greens
Do we even look at what's to be seen?
It must sadden God when we get too busy,
always rushing around in some kind of tizzy.
Being so busy it's so hard to live,
and notice the miracles He so gladly gives.

So many miracles go unnoticed. Our King prepares them for His children, and we walk through our day unaware. How this must hurt Him. We can almost hear

Him say: "I made this rose in your garden smell extra sweet, and I mixed its color just for you. You never even noticed it had opened. Well, maybe tomorrow."

- Spring, when He allows His sleeping trees to awake and revive, as they again cover the earth with their beauty.
- Winter, when He has so much fun preparing a snowfall. Each of His zillions of snowflakes are all unique and different. Now, isn't that just like His Majesty?
- Autumn, colorful, breezy, beautiful autumn when the Master Painter has such fun brushing color all over His world. I can almost imagine Him sitting back on His throne and smiling at the great job He has done. He's even added some brand new color reds this year just for our pleasure, just for His children, His most precious treasures.

His most treasured miracle must be that of a newborn baby, so tiny, so perfectly formed, tiny fingers and tinier fingernails. I wonder if His heart breaks with every little treasure that is aborted. Can you almost imagine the tears running down His face? Again, we have caused Him such excruciating pain, and yet, He still loves us!

Miracles unnoticed everyday, a smile from a stranger, our loving families, and even our not so loving families, our comfortable homes, a special neighbor, a compliment, and even the very air we breathe. Why do we miss these miracles? Are we too busy to see the smile on our child's face? Too busy to get excited over the bean he planted in the paper cup that has finally sprouted and that he's proudly brought home as a gift for you? Too busy to notice God's miracles?

THEN COULD IT BE THAT WE ARE JUST TOO BUSY?

What have you missed today? God has feelings, too, you know!

I love to visit the islands. Their opalescent water, with its graduating shades of blue and turquoise. It never fails to fascinate me. I relish their white sandy beaches and their unique island foliage. However, when talking with the island's inhabitants, I mentioned my enthusiasm over the beauty I found there. They smiled and casually told me that they hardly even notice the beauty as they live with it every day.

Perhaps this is why we miss seeing so much of what Our Majesty has prepared for us. Our eyes have become accustomed to His everyday love for us, but, does God ever stop His miracles because of our indifference? Not on your life. He closes each day with a gorgeous sunset, then a sky full of diamonds, and then He says, "Tomorrow I'll add more blue to the sky for them. Tomorrow I'll try harder. Tomorrow they will see." Take a real good look around your world tomorrow and maybe, just maybe, you'll be able to see some beautiful "Glimpses of His Majesty."

Why do we take God for granted? Why do we expect so much and give so little? We spend so much on our new car, and yet we reluctantly drop a few dollars into the collection plate. We put on our brand new suit for an interview, but we put on a casual shirt and pair of slacks to worship our creator on Sunday.

Why do we meticulously clean our homes when company is coming, and yet not care about the immoral magazines we've tucked under the coffee table? Would we ever be surprised if our Lord dropped in for a surprise visit, (I sure hope I tucked them under that table far enough)

Do we take Him for granted because we know how He loves us, because He is so eager to forgive us, or is it that He stands very silently, (without making any waves), at the door of our hearts? Perhaps it's because He has showered us with so many gifts that we have come to expect them. Maybe it's because we expect Him to answer our prayers and He does, or is it because our life is going okay right now and we feel we really don't need Him. Maybe we'll just put Him in our pocket until we do.

"HIS CRYSTAL WORLD"

We went to sleep last night while the snow was
coming down.
The wind was blowing big white drifts, you couldn't
see the ground.
We tucked ourselves in warm and tight,
Snug as could be on a cold winter's night.
Unaware of the miracles happening outside.
Every so often He allows us to see
A miracle so lovely it's hard to believe.
Icy snow turned to rain, turning flakes into diamonds,
The trees into crystal, the streets into glass.
God waited till morning, making it last.
He waited excited to see all our joy,
The "oohs" and the "ahs" and all the "oh boys"!
A world made of crystal for all to see,
He laughed and said, "I did it all for thee."
I looked at the crystal branches raised high,
As if they were praying up to the sky.
A miracle so lovely I just had to say,
Thank you, Your Majesty, for your fine crystal day.

§

God calls His people to Him in so many ways.
Who knows what touches another's heart? Sometimes
it's music and sometimes it's nature.

The bride and groom were so happy. The wedding
feast was going perfectly when Mary overheard the
wedding master whisper to the servants that the wine
was almost gone. He had underestimated the amount
needed. This was an unforgivable mistake, and would

be an insult to the groom and his bride. Mary realized what she had to do. She approached Jesus and told Him that the wine was almost gone. Jesus kindly, but hesitatingly, looked at her and said, "Woman, what have I to do with this? My time has not yet come." Was Jesus being disrespectful to His mother? Not at all, this was the customary answer of a son to His mother in that time. Jesus' heart was filled with so much love for her that He obeyed her. By turning those thirty-gallon jugs of water into wine, He took the saddest step He would ever take. The cross loomed hauntingly in the foreground. By performing His first miracle, He also took His first step toward His cross. He knew there would be no turning back for Him. No turning back to those warm comfy nights as He slept on His mat in the loft over Mary's oven. Even the coldest of Nazareth's nights found Him toasty warm.

He was destined never to have a home of His own, and many nights He could be found sleeping on the cold, damp ground of Gethsemane. Sometimes in a heavy rain, He and His followers would seek shelter in one of the damp caves that had been hewn out of the rock in the garden.

No turning back to all the fun He had with His friends from the Synagogue and back in Nazareth. His life would now be very busy going about His Fathers business as well as moving step-by-step toward the job He came to do.

Gone would be His comfort and His privacy, and how He must have missed Mary's good cooking. There would be many times when He would ache from hunger. He who made the world and all it contains would sometimes have to depend on the kindness of others for food.

No wonder He hesitated to perform that first miracle. He knew with the obedience to His mother, His days on this earth were shortened, His purpose in coming was heightened, His life would never be the same, but above all else, He knew there would be no turning back. His walk to His Cross had begun this very evening.

HE IS ALWAYS WITH US

Terry and Brian began setting the table for dinner. Terry usually set the table and Brian did the dishes. Their dad sat and read his papers. Sometimes he would bring his wife dinner if her stomach could take it. Mrs. Falco had been sick for a few years now, but only the last few months had she been confined to bed. Terry, Brian, and their dad were aware of Mrs. Falco's cancer. They had watched her getting weaker and weaker by the day. They spent lots of time with her, but sometimes she was so tired that it was difficult for her to talk. Brian was especially angry. Where was God now? Didn't his Sunday school teacher say, He was always with us? Brian was very upset with God right now.

The door rang. It was Mrs. Brooks with a huge casserole for tomorrow nights' supper. Mr. Falco thanked her and said goodbye.

Brian's dad began opening today's mail, sorting out cards for his wife and lots of bills. As Mrs. Falco opened her cards, she would smile, and some she would hold to her chest. She always seemed to enjoy this so much. As

Brian watched her opening her mail, his eyes seemed to open too! Why, God really was there. He was there in the cards his mom received every day. He was there in Mrs. Brooks as she brought them her wonderful casseroles. He was there with the ladies in the church who volunteered their help to clean the house every week. And how about the neighbors who did their food shopping and wouldn't even accept payment for it no matter how hard his dad tried to make them take it.

Now, Brian understood what Mrs. Lakey said last week in Sunday school. "Even though you can't see Him, God is still there. Kind of like not being able to see the wind, but you know it's there." Brian apologized to God just before going to bed. He knew, too, that God would be here for all of them in the difficult days ahead.

§

SPRING IS COMING

Jerry looked out at his acreage that surrounded the home Sarah's dad left them when he passed away. He and Sarah had done a great job of fixing up the house. It was a dream come true for both of them, but since Sarah was no longer there to enjoy it with him, the excitement had gone out of his life.

Sarah had gone for a normal checkup. The doctor had ordered some tests to be done. The tests revealed a rare liver disease. Additional tests showed that Sarah's disease was too far advanced for her to be helped. This probably explained the slight yellow tinge on her skin the last few months.

The doctors were able to keep her comfortable, but on a rainy morning just before Christmas, she went home to the Lord. Jerry was devastated. Other than feeding the horses and caring for the farm, there was no joy in his life. How could he go on without Sarah?

It was an unusually warm spring morning. He carried his coffee out to the back porch to sit for a few minutes. He blinked a few times. His eyes could not believe what he was seeing. Color was everywhere. What had happened? There were crocuses everywhere, hundreds of them. Suddenly he knew. This explained the note that he found from Sarah. She had left it in his bureau drawer along with his socks. The note said: "Look for me in the spring." She knew he would be lonely, so in the fall she had planted hundreds of crocuses as a goodbye gift to him. The whole colorful back yard seemed to say "Life goes on." Life is a gift, I love you, and I want you to go on and enjoy it. He suddenly felt that he could go on, as he knew he would see her gesture of love for him come alive again every spring.

§

HIS MAJESTY'S MIGHTY HAND

My husband and I had the pleasure of taking a cruise to Bermuda. On our second day out to sea, I pushed back the curtains in our room to look at the ocean before us. It was everywhere the eye could see, unbelievably beautiful, and it looked overwhelmingly powerful. Here was I, first hand, gazing at God's handiwork. I could almost see His Majesty's mighty hand reaching over the waters, separating them from dry land and lovingly whispering to them their boundaries, placing His magnificent mighty hand over them and telling them to go no farther. Yes, He had been here over just these waters, and I felt safe and loved. He hides me in the shadow of His hand. Isaiah 49:2 For God, His Mighty Majesty loves me, and He loves you too!

§

When our children were young, we spent many happy days on the seashore. They seemed to inherit my love for it. Packing everything up was a major problem, but once we got there, I always thought it was worth the effort. One day, my youngest daughter, with her pail in hand, went out to fill it up with water. She yelled for me to come help her with the pail because it was too heavy. As I went to help her, reality set in. Here was just a pail of water and it was heavy. Could anyone imagine the combined weight of all the oceans in our world as it hangs suspended in space? We will have to leave it to "His Majesty," for with Him "All things are possible." Mark 10:27

CHAPTER 4

IT'S NOT EASY "BEING HUMBLE"

Humility is Christian love. It always seeks the last place. It always fights that battle of selfishness, egoism, taking time from yourself to be of service to others. Humility goes a long way with poverty. When one is poor, he must rely on God for everything. E. Stanley Jones tells of a poor man who had an overnight guest. As he showed him to his humble bedroom in the hayloft, he said, "If there is anything you want, let us know, and we will come and show you how to get along without it."

We don't need to learn how to get more, but how to get along with what we've got, and how to get on with the business of living and loving. Sometimes possessions can possess the man.

True godliness is achieved not by elevating ourselves but by lowering ourselves.

Take a good look at yourself, and you will look at others differently.

By humbling ourselves in prayer, we can know how lowly and sinful we are, and how almighty Our God is!

The man who desires honor does not deserve it.

True humility and respect for the Lord lead a man to riches, honor, and long life.

Better to be poor and humble than prideful and rich.
Proverbs 16:19

When we forget ourselves, we usually start doing things others will remember.

§

HUMILITY IS:

- Putting aside personal pride
- Standing in the background without feeling hurt
- Setting aside any self-importance of ones self
- Giving time to a friend in need when your time is so limited
- Always putting others before yourself

Humility is perpetual quietness of heart. It is never to be fretted or vexed, irritable or sore, to wonder at nothing that is done against you. It is to be at rest when nobody praises you or when you are blamed. It is to have a blessed home within yourself where you can go in and shut the door, kneel to your "Father" in secret and be at peace as in a deep sea of calmness, when all around and about there is turmoil. It's really not easy to be humble.

CAN PEOPLE SEE THAT THERE IS SOMETHING DIFFERENT ABOUT YOU?

- Can they see joy on your face?
- Can they see your Colgate smile?
- Have you ever let that person with only one item step in front of you at the supermarket?
- Have you thanked anyone today, the mailman, the grocery bagger?
- How about that elderly neighbor next door? You're going shopping, does she need milk or eggs, etc?
- How about garbage night, have you ever thought that lifting those heavy cans to the curb might be difficult for her?
- What about that someone trying to get on the entrance ramp? Did you slow up to let him on, or did you step on the gas? {maybe just a little bit}

Such little gestures, but wasn't Christ kind? Didn't He take the time to touch, to teach, to smile at the children, to stop and talk to people, to help whenever He could? He cared, and He showed it. So what is our problem? Are we too busy to show someone we care, or is it that we really don't care? Is it that we are too busy to stop and help? Then guess what? WE ARE JUST TOO BUSY!

Remember, you may be the only example of Jesus Christ another person ever sees. Humble yourself to help others.

When we come into God's presence with open hearts and hands, this is prayer. All that we cling to disappears when our hands are opened. If we are willing to wait with open hands, He will come! When we wait humbly before Him, it is then that He knows He is all-important in our lives. By opening our hearts and hands, we are totally surrendering to Him.

Prayer is knowing we are loved exactly as we are, and simply letting yourself be loved by God. It is a humble, gentle waiting for Him.

§

GOD LOVES HUMILITY

His Whole life was one of humility.

Have I the right to own a home, when my Savior had none?

To have so many friends when His friends deserted Him?

To be able to shop for food whenever I like, when many times He was hungry?

To sleep in my own comfortable bed, when many nights He slept on the cold, damp ground?

To be able to drive anywhere I want, when Jesus walked the dusty roads in sandals?

To have a much varied wardrobe, when Jesus had only the clothes on His back?

To have so many creature comforts, while Jesus had none? Material things were unimportant to Him.

Lord, let materialism be as unimportant to me as it was to you. Don't store up treasures here on earth where they can erode away or may be stolen. Store them in heaven where they will never lose their value, and are safe from thieves. If your profits are in heaven your heart will be there too. Matthew 6:19-21 Do I need so many clothes? Half of them I haven't worn in years anyway. Do we need a dessert after dinner every night? And how about teddy bears? (Oh! How I love teddy bears), but do I need twenty of them?

§

Only when we have nothing, can we look to His Majesty for everything.

Never let gold become your God.

The plenty of heaven will more than compensate for the poverty of earth.

How empty is the life that is filled with nothing but things.

We are not made rich by what is in our pockets but only by what's in our hearts.

A selfish heart loves for what it gets. A humble heart loves for what it can give.

§

I LIVED FOR MYSELF

I lived for myself and thought of myself
Myself and no one beside
Just as if Jesus had never lived
And if He had never died

§

HUMILITY IN ACTION

His birthplace, a stable cave,
The breath of the animals kept Him warm.
His cradle, a feeding trough,
His people denied Him, they tried to kill Him.
He was homeless and hungry.
He was sometimes tired and dirty.
His own town folk didn't believe in Him.
A friend sold Him for the meager price of a slave.
(He owned everything that eye could see, but the
clothes on His back were his only possessions.)

§

He gave up His heavenly home to become one of us,
but His ultimate act of humility took place on the site
of a garbage dump outside the city of Jerusalem (the
city He loved so much) "Golgatha and His cross"!

His entire life from beginning to end was one of utter
humility. And—It pleased the father that it was so!

Every time we open our mouth we have a choice to make, to encourage, to uplift, to give hope or to undermine, to discourage, to judge (no matter how slightly.)

Doesn't it take just as much time to be nice than it does to be nasty?
If my people will humble themselves and pray, and turn from their wicked ways, I will hear them from Heaven and forgive their sins and heal their land. I will listen, wide awake, to every prayer made in this place. 2 Chronicles 7:14-15

CHAPTER 5

HE CAME TO PAY A DEBT HE DIDN'T OWE, BECAUSE WE OWED A DEBT WE COULDN'T PAY

It was a cold, crisp night. There were so many stars. They seemed so close that the shepherds on the hillsides felt like they could almost touch them. Their flocks were unusually content this evening. The shepherds felt this contentment too.

Along the dusty road below them, unnoticed, came three weary travelers, a man bent over from exhaustion, a very young woman who was soon to deliver her child, and one tired, dirty, but grateful donkey, for on his back he carried God's Son. If you looked carefully, you would be able to see how cautiously this donkey stepped. He was being overly cautious so as not to step in any holes in the road, or stumble on the many rocks that were embedded everywhere. As tired as he was, he was trying to make this burden of a journey as comfortable as possible for Mary. As weary as she was, he had not heard her complain. So many things were running through her young mind. Would the delivery be painful? Would Joseph be able to help if the delivery was difficult?

Yes, Mary was to be truly blessed. She would be the first human being to look into the face of God! She would hear His first word, watch Him carefully as He took His first step. She had no idea how much sadness would be mingled with her joy.

Did anyone seem to care that God came into the world this night? The inn was full, (or so they said). Everyone in this Bethlehem town was much too occupied to know or even to care about this infant king. How sad! No room for Him in the world He made. And—no room for Him in the hearts that He made.

A night full of stars, a cold, dark night,
A cautious husband, a tired wife,
A journey's end, a donkey's strife,

The inn was full, or so they said.
They needed to rest, to lay their heads.
"A cave", said the innkeeper, "where the animals stay,
They would keep you warm, and there's plenty of hay."

Joseph said yes, for Mary was due.
To have God's Son, would a stable do?
Did the animals smile when they opened the door?
Could they possibly have known what this night held in store?
They knew they were blessed but didn't know why.
They had been chosen to hear "HIS" first cry.

A place in the hay was prepared in haste.
For Mary knew there was no time to waste.
Was that star overhead "THE MOST HOLY ONE?"
Watching over the birth of His most-precious Son?

The miracle of miracles happened that night.
When "Heaven" came to earth and turned darkness to
light!

§

Did anyone even bother to clean the dung out of
the stable to get the stench out? Was the hay He laid
on even clean? No one would ever have suspected that
"He", who made the sun to warm the earth, would one
day have need of an ox and an ass to warm Him with
their breath. His golden throne was traded for a dirty
sheep trough.

How humble this precious, helpless little lamb,
(known in heaven as "HIS MAJESTY") was struggling
to work His never-before used lungs. How weak He
was, for now He had limits. In "His" heavenly home
"He" knew no limits, no boundaries, no illness, no
hate, and no hunger. These would all be new to Him.
These were all part of the price He paid to become one
of us. These were all part of the price He paid to save
us. He limited Himself to depend totally on others,
having to be fed, having to wear diapers, learning how
to talk, how to walk, scraping His knees when He fell,
and depending on others to comfort Him. How could
we ever understand a love like this? Even as a baby,
did Jesus know why He had come? He was fully God
and fully man. He knew!

Rest, your little "Majesty." Rest in Mary's warm
arms, for soon you will be called on to do the painful
job you were born to do, the job of saving "me."

His tiny baby "God hands" touched Mary's cheek.
Those hands would someday mercifully reach out to

touch the dreaded leper, would touch a dead teenager and give him back to his mother, would open blind eyes that had never seen colors or trees or the beloved faces of his wife and children. But—for now "He" was safe and warm.

Out on the hillsides tens of thousands of angels, as well as the "Heavenly Host" praised Him. They sang until the thin streak of dawn broke through the darkness.

All the pieces of this beautiful plan fit together so perfectly if we just take the time to look at it.

He appeared first to the shepherds. He was to be called "The Good Shepherd."

He came humbly to serve and love. Could anything be more humble than a stable cave?

The gifts that the Wise Men brought Him were gifts of:

- Frankincense—an incense He would need in celebrating His Jewish customs.
- Myrrh—a costly ointment that was used to prepare the burial wrapping cloths wound around the body.
- Gold—because this tiny baby was truly the "King of Kings."

The excitement of Christmas is everywhere. I have a neighbor who never acknowledges me all year long, but if I meet her in the grocery store during the Christmas holidays, she is all smiles and hellos.

Mothers bake cookies with their children during the holidays, when during the rest of the year they can't seem to find the time.

Friends come to visit who can't find the time all year long, and they only live two blocks away.

People smile and are much more courteous. They are generous with food and clothes for the needy. Why only on Christmas? I'm sure they like to eat during the rest of the year. Why do we act as "His" heart and "His" hands at Christmas then put Him back on the shelf for another year?

Have you seen "His Majesty? Some will never see Him, not because of blindness, but because even with seeing eyes, they will never look for Him. Will you take the time to find Him? Will you put other things aside and go and find Him? And—when you do, your heart will never let Him go!

Oh sure, we'd like to think that all that junk under the tree that we spent our last dollar on was because of the gifts given to baby Jesus, but it's really because of commercialism, or because the kids saw it on television and are driving us crazy for it. Do some of these children even have a vague idea of what Christmas is all about? We've kind of started this outrageous gift giving all by ourselves. I know what this is like, because when my three children were small, I was guilty of this myself. Christmas is so much more meaningful when we celebrate it for what it truly is. Materialism can be devastating, for the more we have, the more we want.

§

IF CHRISTMAS ISN'T FOUND IN YOUR HEART, YOU WON'T FIND IT UNDER THE TREE
(Charlotte Carpenter)

Christmas is family, Christmas is love.
Christmas is God coming down from above.
So humbly born in a stable cave,
Coming from Paradise, destined to save.

So tiny and small, so helpless "His" form.
He needed the animals to keep "Him" warm.
Mary, looking into her baby's eyes,
Had no idea "He" was destined to die.

It was "God" that she sang to, cuddled and loved,
Humbly coming to us from above.
"He" gave up Paradise to make this "His" home.
What would have happened if "He" had not come?

The gates of Heaven would still be closed tight.
We would still be in darkness, never knowing the
light.
But "God" loved us so, that "He" fashioned a plan.
"He" came to die for the sins of man.

We thank "God" for Christmas and for "His" love;
This most precious baby, "His" gift from above.
We love "Him", we praise "Him", and of "Him" we
sing,
Our "Majesty", "Savior", our "Lord" and our "King."

§

READY FOR CHRISTMAS

"Ready for Christmas," she said with a sigh,
As she gave a last touch to the gifts piled high.
Then wearily sat for a moment to read,
Till soon, very soon, she was nodding her head.
Then quietly spoke a voice in her dream,
"Ready for Christmas, what do you mean?
Ready for Christmas when only last week
You wouldn't acknowledge your friend on the street?
Ready for Christmas while holding a grudge?
Perhaps you'd better let God be the judge.
She woke with a start and a cry of despair.
"There's so little time, and I've still to prepare.
Oh, Father, Forgive me, I see what you mean!
To be ready means more than a house swept clean.
More than the giving of gifts and a tree,
It's the heart swept clean that He wants to see.
A heart that is free from bitterness and sin.
So be ready for Christmas—and be ready for "Him."

CHAPTER 6

THE HIGHEST PLACE OF ALL WILL ALWAYS BE AT THE FOOT OF "HIS" CROSS

E ven as a child, I could always see the beauty in a tree. One of the reasons we bought the home we live in is because of the sturdy row of tall beautiful trees which line the back of our property. Don't you think the fruit tree that tempted Eve in the garden was beautiful (no, the bible doesn't say it was an apple). It says "fruit." Surprised?

Trees can sometimes be ugly, such as the one Jesus died on. It wasn't always ugly. At one time it was beautiful, for Jesus, himself, made that tree. He planted it and nurtured it with tender, loving care. Trees were important to Jesus from the beginning of His life until His death.

- Trees shaded Mary and Joseph's journey into Bethlehem, occasionally affording some well-needed rest along the way.
- A tree formed the animal trough that Jesus slept in as a newborn infant.
- Trees provided the wood that helped Joseph to train Jesus in the carpenter trade.

- Many nights Jesus and His disciples took shelter under the knarled, old olive trees in the Garden of Gethsemane
- Trees provided Jesus with fruit, which sustained Him many times when He ached from hunger.

And—it was a tree that He, Himself, had made, that took his life, which was fashioned into a cross by the cruelest soldiers in the world.

Soldiers, acting as carpenters, would put to death "The Carpenter" who carpented the world.

While working with Joseph, did He ever hit His thumb while hammering a nail? Did He ever think what the pain would be like on the cross as He hammered the nails into pieces of furniture? As He dug the slivers out of His fingers, could He have been thinking of the slivers that would rub against His raw back as He hung on the cross?

He knew it all. He knew why He was sent. He would finish what He came to do. He would look down at those jeering faces He loved so much (the totally unlovable) but, even so, He loved them, and He would finish the job He came to do for them. He would have given even more than His life for them, but that was all He had to give.

ONLY HE WOULD DO

He closed His eyes and saw their tears.
Their cries of anguish filled His ears.

Their doom was certain, this He knew.
For there was nothing they could do.

For Heaven's gates closed long ago.
And Paradise they'd never know.

At night their cries kept Him awake.
Their tear-stained faces made Him shake.

Their begging arms reached out for Him.
He loved them even with their sin.

He knew the pain He would endure.
"THE ONLY WAY" He knew for sure.

For God demanded that only "HE",
Our spotless, sinless, lamb could be.

Only a spotless lamb would do.
To open Paradise for me and you.

§

How often do we say no to our children because it is for their own good? Our Heavenly Father said "NO" to Jesus for the good of the whole world. He loved Jesus, but He loved us more, for each one of us is precious to Him!

Have you ever been hurt by a dear friend? The pain you feel goes right down to your toes. You feel as if your heart is broken. Perhaps this is how Jesus felt when Judas betrayed Him. He had followed Jesus closely for three years. He served as the accountant for the group of disciples, otherwise known as keeper of the moneybag, which he quite often pilfered for his own advantage. Jesus knew it, but He loved him anyway.

Even in the garden when Judas betrayed Him with a kiss, Jesus called him "friend." Friend? This friend sold Him out for the lowly price of a slave. Could this word "friend" have been the deciding factor in Judas hanging himself?

The night before He was crucified, chunks of flesh were taken out of His back. Every prisoner hated that cruel leather whip with the bits of bone and stone at its end. Sticks beating the crown of long thorns into His head (the soldiers had taken them from the long thorn bushes on the hillsides). Spittle all over His face, slaps, punches, and kicks, But we were not there to see what other forms of torture these vicious soldiers could conjure up, what other kinds of pain they could inflict upon Him. His night was filled with every kind of imaginable pain, but—the saddest pain of all was His Father saying "NO" to Him in the garden. His Father had never said no to Him. Jesus knew that His Father was telling Him that there was no other way.

A sadness ran through Him as He remembered His friends deserting Him. Jesus knew these men well. He knew their weaknesses and He knew their strengths, and—He loved them even still! Jesus endured it all patiently, even His fixed trial in which only ninety-eight words were spoken. So much prophecy came true that night.

Not all of His friends deserted Him. Mary Magdalene followed His every step to Calvary. He had set her free, and how she wished she could do the same for Him.

She watched as Jesus fell under the weight of the heavy wooden crossbar. The centurion was eager to get this miserable job done. He had no patience with Jesus' pain. "You there," he pointed to Simon of Cyrene, a pilgrim visitor. "Carry the wood for Him." Mary stood there with tears in her eyes. She would have given everything she owned if only she was strong enough to carry that cross for her beloved Jesus.

Simon thought, "Why me picked out of this huge crowd?" "Just my luck, I guess," but—then Jesus looked at Simon, and Simon could see the love and gratefulness in Jesus' eyes. He knew he had not been given a burden but a real honor, for the man whose loving, bleeding face would ever be before him.

Don't you wish you had been there and the centurion had singled you out to take His burden? Only to Simon went this very precious honor. Simon, you were blessed, but in your heart you knew it didn't you?

Jesus had almost reached the top of the hill. He could see three crosses. Two already had men on them, but the third stake was being lifted out of its place. That one was waiting patiently for Him. As He glanced around, He knew this place well. It was the town garbage dump outside the city where the many carcasses of the sacrificed animals were thrown. Imagine . . . the town garbage dump! The utter humility of our God, being crucified in a garbage dump! The countdown to the job He came to do had just begun.

Blessed are the merciful, but He would be shown no mercy. Scripture states, "Angry dogs surrounded me. "They nailed my hands and feet." Psalms 22:16 What fear He must have felt? If only someone could have thrown his arms around Him and told Him how he loved Him before the first nail was hammered. The sign over His head should have read, "He suffered because He loved."

Although God told Abraham to slay his only son, Isaac, (God was testing Abraham's devotion) He did find another animal sacrifice and spared Isaac. But God could not find another sacrifice for His Son. No other would do. No other was sinless and perfect without a blemish. A perfect God demanded a perfect sacrifice. Only Jesus would do. He really was "The Only Way." Our only way!

To you sin may be a small thing, but to God it is a great and awful thing. It is the second largest thing in the world. Only "God" is greater!
Billy Graham

The sickening smell of blood pervades the hot air and invades your nostrils even before you can see the mass of raw and bloody flesh stretched tightly on the cross. Somehow blood has a sickening smell of copper.

He is covered with blood trickling still from wounds all over His body. Dried blood is matting His hair where the crown of thorns was pressed onto His head. Blood drips down His face. Flies settle on the drying blood. They bite His face, but He is unable to move and shoo them away. No one does it for Him. The sun beats down on Him mercilessly. He writhes in agony within the restriction of the nails. He prays the Psalms. The muscles of His arms and legs are in spasm (just think of leg cramps and multiply them by every muscle in your body.) He could do nothing to stop them. The weight of His body pulls downward, compressing the lungs. He gasps for air! For hours!

The jeering crowd knows no pity even though He is dying the most painful death imaginable. He had cured their sick, cast out their demons, and raised their dead. And even now, He is dying before them to bring them salvation.

The blood dripped down His face and onto His hands; Hands that formed the seas and hands that set its boundaries; Hands that made the sun and moon; Hands that hung the stars; Only the hands of our perfect God would do for this ultimate sacrifice.

Research tells us that the nails were probably driven into His wrists, as the flesh of His hands could not have held His body weight. But—does it really matter where those nails were driven, wrist or hand for the pain was just as great. What really matters is that He said "yes" to all of it and saw it through to the end. He would proudly hold the honor of being called "His Majesty" to the end, when His last words "It is finished" could be heard.

The crowd below Him did not notice the ten thousand angels and the entire Heavenly Host that were waiting in the background should they hear Jesus say "I'm out of here," but those words were never spoken. As Jesus looked out at the faces below Him in the crowd, He also saw those who would be with Him in Paradise, and He knew that this is where He should be and why He had come.

His eyes found His mother. His heart broke as He looked down at her. He saw the tears running down her face. She was once so beautiful, but now she is tired, and the wrinkles on her face show her pain. How He loves her. His heart aches for her. He knows they will both be together again in the not-too-distant future. John supported her arm as he stood next to her. Even now you remember her telling you of something that was said to her when you were a baby. "And a sword shall pierce your soul." Luke 2:34-35 Today this prophecy came true. As you gasped for breath, you gave her to John to care for her in his home until she returned to you. She nodded, sadly, and He knew she understood.

At the foot of His cross they mocked Him saying, "If you are the Son of God, come down from the cross," but because He knew He was the Son of God, He knew he must remain there.

THE RAIN CANNOT SAVE ITSELF IF IT IS TO OPEN THE FLOWERS

You painfully turned your head to the right and then to the left to the two thieves hanging next to you. One wanted you to use your power, (if you were God), to take them down from the cross. But wait—the other one tells you he is sorry and he deserves what is happening to him. He tells the other thief to leave you alone. He asks you to remember him when you come into your kingdom. He really believes in you! He believes you are God! He is why you left your heavenly home, yes, He is why you are hanging there. In your overwhelming pain, you tell him that he will be with you in Paradise. Was this man a gift provided you by your father?

You are thirsty, so thirsty, your blood and water are being drained from your body. Such humiliation, Lord. You hung there naked. They wanted to humiliate you. What more could they do to you? Even so, you forgave them. You forgave them all!

As I look upon your face, dear Lord,
I wonder if it's true?
For no one knows just how you looked,
Were your eyes even blue?

But then a thought occurred to me as I sat and prayed.
What really matters most to me,
Is what you did that day.
Leaving would have been easy,
But you bore the pain and stayed.

So when I look upon your face,
Other things I see.
Your gentle, suffering body dying on the tree for me.

§

The hands that hammered those nails were God's hands. How can we even imagine this? Did God's tears mingle with Jesus' blood as the nails pierced His hands? Can you hear the Father saying, "This is the only way, my Son, They wait at the gate for you." Jesus' last words were "It is finished," but elsewhere, wonderful and exciting things were happening. The dreaded temple curtain, which separated the people from God, ripped itself in two. Those beautiful, heavenly gates, made of a single pearl, flung themselves open wide for the multitudes who had been waiting since the beginning of time, and the thief who hung next to Jesus led them in. Miles and miles of people smiling and laughing together were walking through those gates to eternity.

> It is done, "It is finished", there, at the foot of His cross, His rich red blood, shed for every sin for all time. His blood that forever set us all free.

> The angels waiting in the wings shout "Victory, it is done." Nails couldn't hold Him on that cross. Love did! His love flung open heavens gates forever.

> He came to do what we could not do for ourselves.

> Our debt is stamped "PAID IN FULL".

> He's done it all for us! He asks us only to receive this great gift of eternal life. He asks so little for giving so much.

The nail-pierced hands of Jesus reveal the love-filled heart of God. Love talked about is easily ignored, but when it is demonstrated, it is not easily forgotten.

Father, please keep me ever clinging to the foot of your cross, but most of all, please remind all of us that forgiveness is revisiting the Cross of Christ!

Can a love like this be understood?

No sword could kill it.
No nail could puncture it.
No beating could end it.

A love that asks forgiveness for us because we really did not know what we were doing! Jesus said, "Father, forgive them for they know not what they do." Luke 23:34

I have so many questions that someday when we walk together I will ask Him. Questions too deep for the human mind to comprehend. I know that as we walk through His meadows together, He will answer them all.

"Death is our passing into life"
Make the most of life on earth, but know the very best is yet to come.

§

"SOMEDAY"

I will thank you when I meet you when this painful day
is through.
I will hear your gentle voice say, "I've been waiting
just for you."
He will tell me that He's glad I'm home, and that there's
much to see.
Just being in His presence is quite enough for me.
As we walk through fields of flowers with colors that
are new,
He will tell me, "I've a special place that I've
prepared for you."
As we walk his World of wonders, my eyes have
never seen,
Holding hands and smiling as the good friends we
have been.
The love that I imagined that someday I would see, is
walking right beside me,
Only Him and me!

Among the shoes in my closet they found "THE
HAMMER"
How could they have found it? I thought I had hid it
so well.

Then in between my hangered-dresses fell "THE WHIP"
with its tails ending in bits of bone. And I thought I had
wrapped it around one of the hangers so cleverly and
tucked it away and out of sight.

Going through my drawers, sure enough, they found
them, the ugly, rusty, spike-type "NAILS". I had wrapped

the three of them carefully in three of my scarves. I guess it wasn't carefully enough.

And there, among my hats on the top shelf of my closet, in a bag, they found the "HEAD WREATH OF WOVEN THORNS." You could still see the bits of hair stuck to the dried blood.

They stopped and looked at me then with an ugly accusing look. Then they lifted the final piece of evidence right off my wall. "THE WOODEN CROSS!"

I DID IT! I'M GUILTY! AND—SO ARE YOU!!

§

During the Spanish-American War, Clara Barton was in charge of the work of the Red Cross in Cuba. One day Theodore Roosevelt came to her. He wanted to buy food for his sick and wounded Rough Riders, but she refused to give him any. Roosevelt was angry and upset. His men desperately needed the help, and he was prepared to pay out of his own funds. When he asked someone why he could not buy the supplies, he was told, "Colonel, just ask for it." Roosevelt's face broke out in a smile. Now he understood. The provisions were not for sale. All he had to do was simply ask and they would be given freely.

That is exactly how a sinner receives eternal life. Salvation is a gift that is free for the asking. A millionaire cannot buy it. And there isn't a single thing we can do to earn it! Jesus has done everything that needed to be done, all alone, in a single Friday afternoon ON THE CROSS.

§

Jesus did what all the king's horses and all the king's men couldn't do. He put Humpty Dumpty back together again. He put me and you back together again.

§

"TRUE STORY OUT OF TENNESSEE MOUNTAINS"

Emma was the small town librarian. She had been for forty five years. She knew everyone in town and everyone loved her. She always had a smile for them. She was kind to everyone. She was the town babysitter, and she fed every stray animal she could find. She always brought her famous soup to anyone who was sick. Once, when a family of seven had a house fire, she packed them all tightly into her little home until their home could be rebuilt.

That little home was all Emma had, and she loved it dearly. Her husband had been dead for many years, and now she was alone. She loved coming home after work. She felt safe and happy there. One day, as she was trying to find a book on the ladder, she fell off and broke her leg. She was elderly, and her bones were brittle. Doctors kept her for a week in the hospital and then sent her home.

She had been out of work for four months when she received a letter from the bank. Because she was unable to work, she was also unable to pay her monthly mortgage payments. Her little home was now in foreclosure. Even the banker loved Emma, but there was nothing he could do for her. She had an appointment in one week to sign the papers that would give her home back to the bank. The week went by quickly. A friend picked her up to take her to the bank. Emma's eyes were all red and her friend knew she had been up most of the night crying.

When Emma got to the bank, the banker sat her down, smiled at her, and handed her the mortgage contract which was stamped in bold black letters "PAID IN FULL." She could not believe her eyes. Her debt had been fully erased and fully paid. She sat and cried in sheer delight. The people in town had gotten together and had collected enough to pay the balance of her bill for her! Emma was just stunned to think they would do this for her. Her happiness showed as her tears flowed down her smiling face.

Jesus did the same for us! We deserved to die for our sins for the punishment for sin is death, but Jesus took all of our sins and nailed them to the cross along with those nails in His hands and His feet. Jesus paid our debt for us. Just like Emma's mortgage payment—PAID IN FULL!

PAID IN FULL!!

Thank Him and tell Him you believe it—and then receive it!

ARE YOU FEELING LEFT OUT?

One evening a woman had a dream. Christ was very important to her, and something had been bothering her for quite some time now. She loved her husband. He was really a good man, but he had not yet accepted Christ as his Savior.

Her dream began in a beautiful green meadow. There were flowers and colors that she had never seen before. Everything was unbelievably beautiful. It almost took her breath away.

She watched as her husband walked through this meadow. The scent of the meadow was delightful. She watched as he walked further on.

He could now see a lake which was clear as crystal. He was moving towards a really bright light. Light was everywhere. He could see gold, shimmering gold. Yes, he could see golden thrones!

The woman caught up to her husband. He was so excited! There were three people standing in a line, a woman, another man, and now her husband.

They moved up closer now. He could see a man all in white seated on one of the thrones. The lady in line was smiling at Him. The man on the throne must be Jesus! He felt love like never before. He thought that it must be coming from those eyes. There was such gentleness in them.

The woman went first. She kneeled before Jesus. Jesus placed His hand on her head and said, "Long have I known your love for me." "We will walk in my gardens together."

The beautiful gates opened before her husband as the woman entered in. He could see color everywhere, deep green grass, trees with all kinds of fruit, and most beautiful of all was a gigantic triple rainbow. And then the gates closed.

The man that stood before her husband kneeled before Jesus too. Jesus put His hand on the man's shoulders and said, "You have been my faithful servant, and you have served me well." "Welcome to my Kingdom." Again the gates opened. Her husband could see inside—People were walking and laughing together. Wait—could this be possible? They were walking on gold, streets of pure gold. He remembered his wife telling him something like that. And the music—he had never heard anything so beautiful before. He thought there must thousands of voices.

Again the gates closed. He could hardly wait to get in there. Now he stood before Jesus (his wife watched all this from behind.)

He had never seen such love in a man's eyes, he never thought that a feeling of such love was even possible. He knelt before Jesus like he had seen the others do. Jesus gently put His hands under both arms and lifted him up to face Him. This time he saw love in Jesus' eyes, but he also saw a terrible sadness in them. Was that a tear falling down Jesus' cheek?

Sadly, Jesus said, "You must depart from me, for I know you not!" He felt himself moving away from Jesus. Away from all the beauty and splendor—away from everlasting joy in God's Kingdom, but—worst of all, away from that feeling of perfect love, overpowering perfect love that he never thought could have existed. HE KNEW HE HAD LOST IT ALL.

He would spend eternity in a place of hate, sorrow and unbearable pain! And, worst of all, he knew he would be there forever.

He had never wanted to hear about Jesus. His children and his wife tried to tell him about Jesus, but he was too occupied to hear their message. He had been given so many chances, but he had let Jesus pass by. Jesus was gone forever. There was going to be no second chance. His wife turned away in sadness.

She found herself in bed the next morning. Her husband was in the kitchen making coffee. "Only a dream," she said, and she thanked and praised God! He was still alive! He still had a chance at eternal life! She was going to try so much harder, but she knew it was really her husband's choice. She could only lead him.

Have you led anyone to Christ lately?

Bill thought back to his wonderful summer-school vacations with his uncle Al. He remembered how he loved to visit him. Uncle Al owned a sheep farm, and Bill spent the summers with him helping him with the ranch. Bill knew what he wanted to do with his life at a very young age. He was going to run a sheep ranch of his own. He had saved, worked hard, and finally his dream was going to come true. He had just purchased a ranch. It needed tons of work. The house was a true disaster, but the price was right and little by little he would find the time to repair the house.

He began clearing the land the very next day. He removed all the nettles and poisonous plants that he knew would hurt his sheep. He then set about fencing in his entire property. His sheep would soon arrive from another ranch. He had personally selected and tagged each one of them. They were thinner than he would have liked them to be, but they were healthy. He would see that they were fattened up once they were in his care.

When they arrived, Bill checked each one of them out carefully. He settled them down in the barn with plenty of grain. The barn leaked in numerous places but Bill knew they would be okay for the night. He looked them over proudly as he left them. He planned to have names for each one of them as he got to know them. That night he slept with one eye open and ears strained for any strange noise. He decided to buy a sheep dog the very next day. "Russ" soon became a very important part of Bill's family. Russ was trained to tend sheep since he was a puppy. He would be their constant companion and guard them along with Bill. At least three of the ewes were going to have their lambs soon, and would be easy targets as well as tasty morsels for the constantly-threatening coyotes.

In a very short time, Bill knew his sheep well. They were all gaining weight, and soon he would start on the house which needed a tremendous amount of work. He had fulfilled his promise of giving each one of them a name.

One day when Bill was painting the house, his neighbor stopped by. He was very upset that Bill had put up the fence and was quite loud in letting him know it! Apparently Shawn spent six months out of the year in his Florida home. Bill wondered who cared for the sheep while Shawn was away. Shawn said he kept them in his back pastures when he was away. Bill didn't remember seeing any ranch hands on Shawn's property.

Shawn brought his large herd of sheep home that afternoon. They were in deplorable condition. All Bill could think about was how glad he was that he had the fence separating them from his sheep. He wasn't going to let his sheep get near them. He could not understand how a shepherd could neglect his flock like this? Bill watched over his sheep like a mother hen. They were like his children to him. He had just finished building a large "lean to" which would shelter them from the cold and rain when they were out in the pasture.

Bill could have cried for those sheep of Shawns. He could imagine how they were suffering from parasites. He wondered what Shawn's sheep were thinking as they looked over the fence at the superb condition that his sheep were in.

Shawn didn't care about the sheep at all. There wasn't even shelter for them from the cold winds of winter. He only cared about the small price their sickly little bodies would bring at the slaughterhouse. An entirely different set of shepherds!

One Shepherd loves his sheep as he would his own children, and would probably endanger his own life for their safety. He watched over them with tender care.

The other shepherd considered them a nuisance. He ignored them completely and left them to fend for themselves. They were too sick to run from the ever-present neighborhood coyotes. I think these two shepherds could easily be compared. Bill loved his sheep, watching over them carefully, caring for their welfare, going before them preparing their pasture, and calling each of them by name. Jesus is like this. He watches over us constantly, for we are His children. He goes before us always to prepare our way. He knows each one of us by name, and He even knows the exact number of hairs we have on our heads. The Lord is not only Our Shepherd, he is Our Master, Our Savior, and Our Friend!

Shawn, on the other hand, considered his sheep a bother and a nuisance. Bill saw him kick them out of his way without a second thought. This shepherd never cared a tiny bit for the welfare of his sheep. He never had a kind word for them. Satan is just like this. He hates every one of us. We could never depend on Him to care for us. The Bible tells us in the Book of Job that He is patrolling the Earth to see whom He can devour. He'd sooner see each one of us dead and in his clutches if He could. We have a choice to choose the shepherd of our choice. Jesus gives us that choice because He loves us too much not to. He is God. He could demand that we love only Him, but he loves us too much to do that. A love that is demanded of us could never be true love.

I would be happy with the tiniest corner of your world Lord, if only I could see your face, and, yet you tell me that you are preparing a mansion for me. Isn't this just like "HIS MAJESTY?"

§

Sometimes I go back in time. When I was a child, there was a favorite place I never got tired of. My Uncle George would drive up and beep the horn to surprise my brothers and me. We would fall all over each other trying to get out the door because we all wanted to ride in the rumble seat of his old Ford. It was such fun.

He never had to tell us where we were headed. We knew. It was his favorite place too. We always knew he had packed a superb picnic lunch for us. He made the best corn-breaded fried chicken in the world.

"Mill River," Oh! What a place! It never disappointed us. We played in the Ripley stream for hours picking up pure white round rocks that felt like silk and splashing each other silly. We always knew that Uncle George was keeping a keen eye on us. We loved and trusted him so completely, and we could feel that he loved us just as much. He was always so gentle and patient with us. I don't ever remember him losing his patience or scolding us. We did get kind of loud and obnoxious when we were told to get our things together, but he never did. Sometimes he would point out some of the beauty in the world as we drove. He was my first real glimpse of what I hoped God might be like. I guess what I'm trying to say is that my brothers and I knew that the cross around his neck wasn't just a nice piece of jewelry. He lived his life around that cross. Sometimes, he would even mention Jesus. Why do people get hesitant to speak that name? It was kind of a new thing for us outside of church, but to our Uncle George it wasn't. He made Jesus seem like He was sitting next to us. I am looking forward to seeing my uncle again and being able to tell him what an impact he made on our young lives.

CHAPTER 7

WAS RESURRECTION AN ENDLESS HOPE OR A HOPELESS END?

Have you ever taken the time to walk through an old graveyard? It's kind of spooky but fun too. I can remember making graveyard rubbings with a friend of mine. You put a large piece of paper up against the script on the stone. Then you take a pencil and scribble over the script. We would always go with plenty of sharpened pencils with us. I still have some of those rubbings:

HERE LIES BETTY K. BILLINGS
1826-1869
A FRIEND TO ALL
"DIED IN CHRIST"
"SEE YOU SOON"

AMY G. TERRILL
1830-1873
DIED OF SMALLPOX
"SHE DIED BECAUSE SHE LOVED"
"UNITED WITH CHRIST"

HERE LIES HARLIN AKRON
1820-1864
BELOVED HUSBAND AND FATHER
"WAITING FOR US"

WILLIAM JENNINGS
1818-1862
"HE LOVED NO MAN"
"HE DIED ALONE"

SADEM BELL
1827-1850
"FORGIVEN"

This last inscription always puzzled me. I thought perhaps they had forgotten to finish the rest of the script. But then, in my later teen years I asked Christ into my own life, and then I realized that the word, "FORGIVEN," was really all that mattered in your life. What a weight is lifted from you when you realize that you are without sin. Thank you, Jesus!

Many gravestones carry the inscription, "HERE LIES," but only on Christ's tomb are emblazoned the words, "HE IS NOT HERE." Many good men have lived and died but there is only one man who conquered death—JESUS CHRIST, AND HE WILL LIVE FOREVER!

In G.B Hardy's book "Countdown", he offers thought-provoking questions about the Resurrection:

- Has anyone cheated death and proved it?
- Is it available to me?

Here is the completed record:

1. Confuscius's tomb—occupied
   Budda's tomb—occupied
2. Muhammad's—occupied
3. Jesus's tomb—EMPTY

The Resurrection is a fact not a fable.

The mystery of the Resurrection is what Christianity is all about. It is all too magnificent for us, too glorious for us to understand, but there is one thing that looms over every one of us. Every one of us will someday die. But Jesus tells us to "fear not because He has overcome the world." His Resurrection promises that we no longer need to fear death for the definition of Resurrection is: A life over which death has no power whatsoever. Jesus' promise in John 14:19 tells us, "because He lives, we shall live also." This is a promise that reaches beyond any price put on it, for what price could be put on ETERNAL LIFE?

When we remove Christ's Resurrection, the gospel holds no meaning at all, for the very core of Christianity is gone as well as the core of all our hope.

How can we endure the difficult days before our death in the midst of pain? I had a wonderful friend, who had cancer. She had a piece of paper with this piece of scripture printed on it in large letters so she could see it at the footboard of her bed. It read, "Jesus endured the cross for the joy set before Him." Hebrews 12:2. Her husband added to it, this verse, No mere man has ever seen or imagined what wonderful things God has ready for those that love Him.

Sometimes I think that when I gaze at His face, that will be enough for me, the face of my beloved, "HIS MIGHTY MAJESTY."

Life without Christ is a hopeless end, but life with Christ is an endless hope!! (Billy Graham) There are countless numbers of those who knew Christ, that on their deathbed told of seeing "Heaven open for them," of hearing the most beautiful music they had ever heard. They talked of loved ones who had lost limbs in wars and who they were now seeing whole with limbs restored. Many have mentioned that angels were waiting to take them into His presence. Jesus said, "Because I live, you shall live also." John 14:19

HE'S WAITING

His Majesty is waiting beneath the apple tree.
Across a field of flowers, He waits there just for me.
The closer I get to Him, the more that I can feel,
The love that I have felt for Him is oh! So very real.

He's smiling as I run to Him, and says, "Hello my child."
He takes me in His arms and says, "I've waited quite
awhile."
The love that I am feeling now is love I've never known.
I stay within His loving arms. He tells me, "I'm His own."

I kiss the holes there in His hands, and then His
nail-scarred feet.
I thank Him then for all His gifts, and all He did for me.
I look around and can't believe the beauty that I see.
He smiles and laughs and tells me He's prepared it all
for me.

I tell Him I'm unworthy, and I don't deserve a thing.
Again He smiles and tells me, "I took care of
everything.

§

Little Tina Jennings was on her way home from school. It had been a very difficult day for her. Today was "Tell us about your pet day," but Tina didn't have a pet, and she felt left out. She stood up in class and told everyone why she wanted a pet. She had wanted one of her own for so long.

Tina's family could hardly afford to feed their six children, and a pet was out of the question. They lived in a basement apartment of a tenement building.

As Tina started down the steps, she suddenly stopped. At the bottom of the stairs sat a big fat black cat. Tina walked down the stairs slowly, but the cat did not move. She even purred when Tina ran her hand down her silky, thick, black fur.

Tina called for her mother. Mrs. Jennings opened the door. When she saw the cat, she shooed her away. Tina watched sadly as the cat made a hasty retreat.

Old Mrs. Tenny was watching from her window. Her apartment was just above Tinas. She called Tina to ask her if she would like to feed and play with her canary. Sometimes Mrs. Tenny would tell her stories from the Bible, and then they would make cookies together. As Tina went to get the can of birdseed, Mrs. Tenny went to close her window. Excited, she called Tina to the window. There was the cat coming across the parking lot with a big grey rat dangling out of her mouth. The tenement had been plagued by rats and nothing seemed to get rid of them. Tina ran downstairs to tell her mother. Mr. Jennings heard all the confusion and came to the door. He was excited to see the dead rat. The cat swished her tail and looked up proudly as she dropped the dead rat at his feet.

Tina bent down and picked up the cat, petting and talking to her. Her brothers and sisters were giggling in the background. Mrs. Jennings gave in and told Tina she could make a bed for her under the stairwell. Everyone loved her, and rats were getting very scarce around the tenement.

Tina named her silky because of her soft fur. Silky was very lovable, and she let all the children play with her.

One day as Tina skipped across the parking lot of the tenement, Mrs. Tenny called to her, telling her she had a big surprise waiting for her. She came down to Tinas, and together they went to the furnace room. There on some old rags on a shelf lay silky with seven little kittens. She had gotten into the furnace room when someone opened the door.

At first silky was very protective of those kittens. She would not let anyone go near them, but as they got a little older, she got used to the children playing with them.

Since the rats were gone now, five of the people in her building took kittens. Only two of them were left, and they were getting bigger and bigger. They were beginning to leave the furnace room. Tina always brought them back in.

One day Mrs. Tenny and Tina were baking cookies. When they finished, Mrs. Tenny always went to get her Bible to read to Tina. As she did, she heard growling outside. Tina looked out and saw the two kittens backed up against the fence in the lot. The dog from down the street had them cornered. Tina knew this dog. She saw him everyday on her way home from school as he tried to get off his chain and climb over the fence at her. He must have broken his chain. She ran down the steps and into the lot. Suddenly, a black flash passed her. Silky jumped up and clawed at the dog's eyes. The dog forgot all about the two kittens and attacked silky. Silky fought and clawed the dog, but she was no match for him.

The dog ran away bleeding, but silky lay dead. Tina was crying when mama Jennings came out. Mrs. Tenny comforted Tina and told her she was sorry too. Everyone was!

Tina and Mrs. Jennings rounded up the kittens. Tina's mom told her to pick one out to keep.

When Mrs. Tenny called Tina to come get the cookies they'd baked, she sat her down with a glass of milk so she could talk to her. Tina's eyes were all red from crying.

Mrs. Tenny asked her if she remembered the bible story about Jesus dying on the cross? Silky didn't have to die for her kittens, but she loved them so much that she died to save them. Jesus loved us so much that He died to save us too. He died to pay for our sins so we wouldn't have to suffer and die for them.

I think I understand now, Mrs. Tenny," said Tina. I'll try to take good care of Silky's kittens for her.

CHAPTER 8

"NOTHING COSTS AS MUCH AS "LOVING" EXCEPT "NOT LOVING"

He will collect your tears in a bottle with your name on it! Each individual tear is precious to Him. Psalms 56:8

Even though love sometimes brings pain and sorrow, what would life be without it?

When we find it hard to forgive others for hurting us, let your mind search out the cross and Jesus will show you what forgiveness really is.

I have branded you on the palm of my hand. Isaiah 49:16 God never looks at His hand without seeing you and me!

§

In one of the battles of the civil war, when his army was suffering a severe defeat, General Lee rode over a section of the battlefield where the fighting had passed on. As he did so, a wounded enemy soldier, in the spirit of defiance, lifted his head and shouted, "Hurrah for the Union."

The soldier then expected to be shot, but instead, General Lee dismounted and knelt beside him and said,

"I'm sorry that you are so gravely wounded. I hope you will soon be well."

Afterward, the soldier said, "His kindness broke my heart, and I cried myself to sleep."

When you choose to love your enemies, they no longer exist.

Hatred breeds hatred, but love creates love.

Those who deserve love the least, are those who need it the most.

§

When we hear about the unconditional love of Jesus, what does that mean to us? It simply means that He accepts you exactly the way you are with no exceptions:

- We can do nothing on our own to merit Jesus' love.
- He loves us whether we are lovely or have a face only a mother can love.
- He loves us no matter what we do or what we leave undone.
- He loves us whether we are prosperous or poor, fat or thin.

In the eyes of God, you are His most prized possession. He made you for His pleasure. You are His very special treasure. As a matter of fact, you are "The apple of His eye." Psalms 17:8

God never gives up on us, even if we completely reject Him. His love never changes, it is always the same. But He hopes and waits patiently for the day that you realize that He is there. When you realize how badly you need Him and you surrender your life to Him.

Some of us are afraid that surrendering our life to Him would mean changing our life around. Would a God who gave His life for you ever give you anything that would make you unhappy? Let's be honest, some of us could really use a change for the better. He would never invade your life. He doesn't work that way. He comes gently, and with much love as He touches your heart.

Some hear His voice, but few open the door. Some even close the door in His face, but—He will try again because He loves them.

Can you imagine them dancing in the streets of Heaven when you finally say "yes" to Him? And—everyone will be celebrating just for you! It's party time in Heaven!

David Needham, in his book "Close to His Majesty" explains love this way. It was a warm summer day. You borrowed the glass from the desk drawer and took it outside in the sunshine. Then you held it at just the right distance to form a tiny circle of brilliant light in a small pile of dry grass or leaves. (Maybe you were just mean enough to aim that spot at the opening of an anthill.)

In a few moments it began to smoke, then burst into flame. Somehow that glass lens was able to gather the rays of sunlight, directing the combined sizzling intensity to that one spot.

Now picture the world, a globe covered with billions of people, and above it, like rays from the sun, the blinding intensity and the wrath of God bearing down upon the human race. Then imagine a great cosmic magnifying glass, as wide as the world, placed in between, gathering all that sizzling intensity of burning wrath and focusing it on one spot. Focusing it on one individual, on Jesus nailed to the cross.

It could have been like a drop of sizzling hot acid dropped on Jesus from above, but instead, it was nails and a cross. Jesus let them do it, and when they finished, He even forgave them. Now that's love. Could we ever even begin to understand a love like that?

§

How often have you met a gentle, caring person? One who seems concerned with only you? He listens to you intently. This person is usually quiet and seems very relaxed. He or she has a gentle attitude in all he or she does or says. If you have ever met someone like this, chances are that this person has stayed on your mind because of the impression he or she made on you. Jesus was confident in the Father's love. This produced in Him a gentle and patient spirit. Faith usually produces an attitude that is relaxed and loving. We can rest comfortably knowing we have accepted His love for us and that we are His children.

He tells us that He will shelter us under His wings. Psalms 91:4 (one of my favorites)

He tells us that He will hold me in the palm of His hand. Isaiah 49:16

We can be sensitive to the needs of others, lending a sympathetic ear when needed. Sometimes others just need to vent their hurts to feel better. Being gentle should never be confused with weakness. Some of the gentlest people I know are some of the strongest Christians I know.

Thank you Jesus, for doing for me in a single Friday afternoon what I could not have done for myself in a million years!

I had spent much time in prayer for someone I loved. Someone who was in deep trouble and needed much help. My prayers were answered over and above all I had asked. In thanking Jesus, I told Him I was going to do all I could do to live a perfect life.

I really did try hard, but Monday morning came along with a flat tire. I was going to be late to work. (Did an unhealthy word or two enter my mind?)

And how was I to know that Betty would be passing around pictures of her large and beautiful new home? (Did I detect some jealousy here?)

My boss called me in the afternoon asking for the completion of a job I had been given, I told him I was just finishing up on it. I hadn't had time to even start it. (Just a little white lie)

Getting home later than usual and noticing that others hadn't made an attempt to start dinner had me venting my feelings quite loudly (where was that patience a Christian should have?)

Only one day and I had failed Him. I realized then that it was impossible for me to ever hope or even try to be perfect. But then—if I could be perfect, would Jesus have had to come at all?

And even when I slip and fall, He tells me that underneath He will catch me in His everlasting arms. Deuteronomy 33:27 He loves me! He has told me so!

> Just let me take a moment to dwell in my savior's arms.
> To know that I am safe with Him, away from any harm,
> And when I'm tired and weary as a busy life does bring,
> It's then I go to run and hide in the shadow of His wings.

§

Jim Lovell, one of our Apollo astronauts, (looking back on earth), tells of our planet as being whole, round, beautiful and small, a blue, green, and tan globe totally suspended in space.

Reflecting on the scene later, He said, "It was just another body about four times bigger than the moon but it held all the hope, all the life, and all of the things that the crew of the Apollo 8 knew and loved. It was the most beautiful thing there was to see in all the heavens. Complete and totally suspended in space. Can you imagine seeing this? Nothing is too difficult or even impossible for "His Majesty."

§

THE TRUE MEASURE OF GOD'S LOVE IS THAT HE LOVES WITHOUT MEASURE

His patience never waivers as He waits there by the door.
His love is oh, so patient, and He'll wait forevermore.

Oh! He could push His way right in, but this He'd
never do,
Because He loves you so very much, He leaves that
up to you.

And so He waits, and waits, and waits, He'll never
leave your door.
And as He waits, He'll shed some tears, just hoping
you will see,
Your time is getting shorter, your twilight soon to be.

He wants to give you all He has to claim you as His child,
For He's been waiting all these years so gentle and so
mild.

So open the door and invite Him in. He's waited oh so
long.
He'll rush right in and hold you in His loving arms awhile.
Then holding out His hands, he'll say, "I did this for
you my child."

§

It seems I can always find Him in the book of
PSALMS. They have a special place in my heart, for
He is always there waiting for me ready to hide me in
the shadow of His wings! Psalms 63:6

"HIS MAJESTY"
"I AM THAT I AM"

God said to Moses, "I am that I am." Thus shalt thou say unto the children of Israel, "I AM" has sent me unto you.

I AM your lord and your God.
ISAIAH 41:10

I AM your comfort and your joy.
PSALMS 16:11

I AM the God of your salvation.
PSALMS 27:1

I AM Alpha and Omega, the beginning and the end.
REVELATION 1:8

I AM the Bread of Life.
JOHN 6:35

I AM everlasting love and truth.
JEREMIAH 31:3

I AM He that holds the keys to Heaven and Hell.

I AM your God who healeth thee.
LUKE 13:32

I AM the Word which abideth forever. And the Word was God.
1 JOHN 1:1

I AM the same today as I was yesterday and will be forever. HEBREWS 13:8

I AM with you always even unto the end of the world. MATTHEW 28:20

I AM The good shepherd. I give my life for the sheep. JOHN 10:11

I AM The Way, The Truth, and The Life. JOHN 14:6

I AM your strength and your portion forever. PSALMS 73:26

I AM perfect righteousness. His righteousness endures forever. PSALMS 111:3

I AM the Light Of Men. JOHN 1:1-4

I AM He who made the heavens and all the host of them by the breath of my mouth. PSALMS 33:6

I AM faithful unto all generations. PSALM 119:90-91

I AM Truth, and the truth will set you free. JOHN 8:32

I AM gentle and kind and slow to anger. MATTHEW 11:29-30

I AM with thee wherever thou goest.
JOSHUA 1:9

I AM faithful in all my promises.
JOSHUA 119:49-50 also 2 CORINTHIANS 1:20

I AM their God, and they shall be my people.
JEREMIAH 7:23

I AM your refuge and your strength, your ever-present help in time of trouble.
PSALMS 31:14-15

I AM your guide, your God forever, even unto death.
PSALMS 48:14

I AM ALL YOU WILL EVER NEED!

The Israeli People Called Him "EL SHADDEI" Which Means: All You Will Ever Need.

HE IS "LORD", HE IS "OUR ETERNAL ALMIGHTY "KING", ALSO KNOWN AS:

"HIS MIGHTY MAJESTY"

NOTES

ABOUT THE AUTHOR

The author lives in Connecticut with her husband. They have three grown children. She has attended a number of theological seminars and a number of classes in advanced biblical studies. Her love for Jesus just leaps off the page!